MY MAGIC BOOK

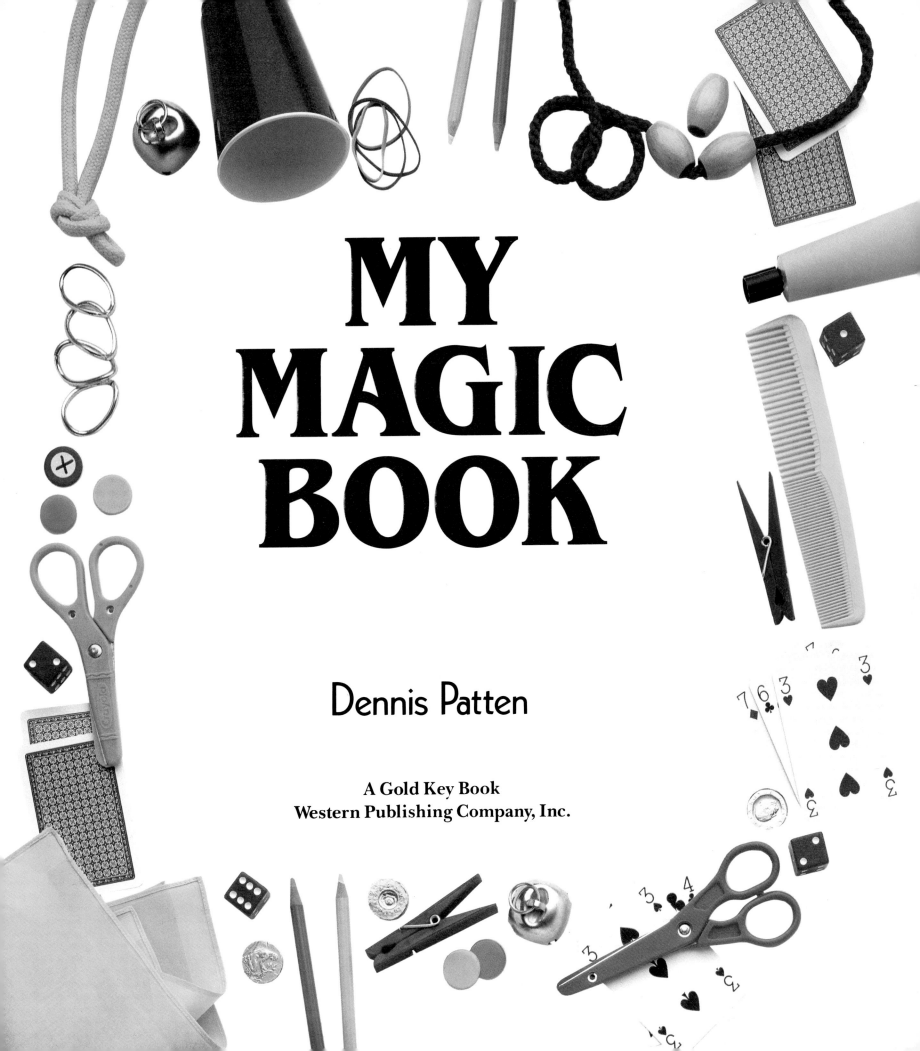

MY
MAGIC
BOOK

Dennis Patten

A Gold Key Book
Western Publishing Company, Inc.

The publishers would like to thank Leslie Thompson, educational consultant, and Philip
Klipper, magic consultant, for their help and advice in compiling this book.

CONTENTS

INTRODUCTION

If you would like to learn how to be a magician, then *My Magic Book* is just for you! It's crammed full of amazing tricks and useful tips on how to perform your own magic show, as well as ideas for making essential props, such as a top hat and a magic wand. All the tricks are easy to do, and range from simple coin and card tricks to "levitating" an assistant for your Grand Finale.

Be very careful when using sharp scissors!

BEFORE YOU BEGIN

- Read through the trick before you start in case you need some help from an adult.
- Assemble all the items you will need before you begin.
- Cover the work surface with newspaper or an old cloth if you need to use paint or glue.

WHEN YOU HAVE FINISHED

- Tidy everything away. Store special pens, paints, glue, etc., in old ice-cream containers or coffee cans.
- Find a secret place to keep your tricks hidden so no one can find them and discover how you do your magic.

SAFETY FIRST!

Use your common sense when using anything sharp like scissors or needles. You will be able to prepare most of the tricks yourself, but sometimes you may need help. Look out for the SAFETY TIP. It appears on those projects where you will need to ask an adult for help.

Please remember the basic rules of safety:

- Never leave scissors open or lying around where smaller children can reach them.
- Always stick needles and pins into a pincushion or a scrap of cloth when you are not using them.

Practice your tricks in front of a mirror until you can do them smoothly and easily.

Get everything ready before you start, and don't forget to clean up afterward.

EQUIPMENT

Every project will list all the things you need; for many of them, you will simply need to hunt around the house. Some tricks call for items, such as a pack of playing cards or a silk scarf, that you may need to buy if you do not already have them. You should be able to find everything you need at a department store, magic shop, or toy shop.

MAGIC WORDS

When you perform a magic trick in front of your audience, you may want to say some magic words or an incantation (a set of words to be said when casting a magic spell). Magicians have always used words like "Abracadabra!" to add an element of surprise and mystery to the show. Why not think up a special set of words for each trick beforehand? The choice of words is yours.

PUTTING ON A SHOW

Before you are ready to put on a show, you will need to rehearse the tricks until you can do them smoothly and easily. Practice in front of a mirror and, when you think you are ready, try the tricks out on a friend. It is also important to look the part for your show. On the following pages you will find instructions for making a top hat and a magic wand. Before you start your show, introduce yourself to your audience and explain what you are going to do—without giving away any secrets, of course! Then all you need to do is perform the tricks and wait for the applause.

GROWN-UPS TAKE NOTE

The tricks in *My Magic Book* need a minimum of adult supervision. However, some potentially dangerous items such as sharp scissors do need to be used occasionally. Your involvement will depend on the ability of the child.

MAGIC WAND

One of the most important items a magician needs is a magic wand. It's very easy to make your own wand out of newspaper, and you can paint it any color you like.

1 Take a sheet of newspaper and roll it up as tightly as possible, as shown above. Try to keep the edges straight.

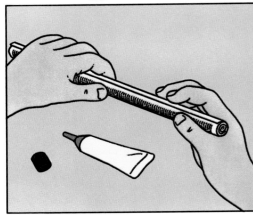

YOU WILL NEED

Newspaper
All-purpose glue
Scissors
Poster paints and paintbrush

2 Spread a line of glue along one long edge of the newspaper and glue it to the rolled-up section. Apply pressure until the paper is firmly stuck in place.

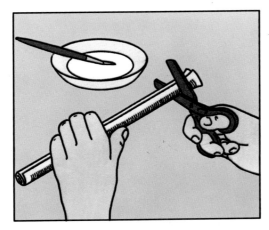

3 Carefully trim the ends of the wand with scissors. Paint the tips white using poster paint.

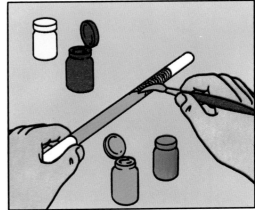

4 Paint the middle section of the wand in a color of your choice. Leave the wand in a safe place until the paint has dried. Alternatively, you can cover your wand in shiny giftwrap paper.

MAGICIAN'S TOP HAT

Every magician needs a top hat to wear and use in performances. They can be expensive to buy, so try making your own from black poster board. Decorate the hat with shiny stars and you will look like a real professional.

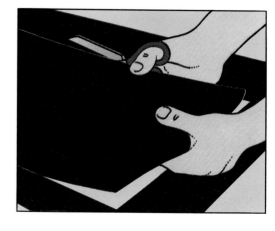

1 Cut out a strip of black poster board long enough to go around your head and about 8¼ inches wide.

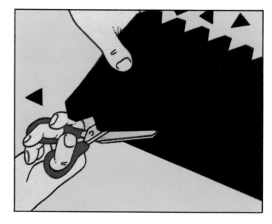

2 Cut tabs along both long edges of the strip, as shown. Form the strip into a cylinder. Stick the ends together with tape on the inside.

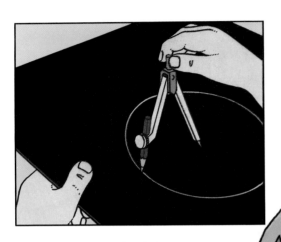

3 To make the brim, measure the diameter of the cylinder across the top of the hat with a ruler. Set your compasses to half this measurement and draw a circle this size on the remaining poster board.

YOU WILL NEED

Black poster board
A ruler
Pair of compasses
Scissors
All-purpose glue
Shiny stick-on stars

4 Keep the point of the compasses in the same place and draw another circle 2 inches larger than the first. Carefully cut around both circles to make a ring. This is the brim of the hat.

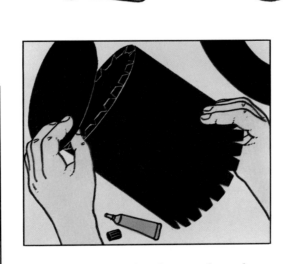

5 Cut a circle of poster board to fit the top of the hat. (The leftover from the brim may fit.) Bend down the tabs at the top of the cylinder and coat them with glue. Stick the circle to the tabs. Trim the edges.

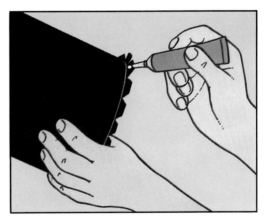

6 Bend the tabs at the bottom of the cylinder up and coat the tops with glue. Slide the brim over the cylinder and stick to the tabs. Cut another circle of poster board and glue it to the bottom of the brim to hide the tabs and strengthen the brim. To finish, decorate the hat with stick-on stars.

THE BOOK OF SPELLS

No magic show would be complete without a magic wand for weaving spells. Your audience will gasp in amazement as you conjure up your trusty wand out of a book of secret spells. Only you will know that the wand was up your sleeve all the time! Practice this trick in front of a mirror to get your moves smooth and the angles right.

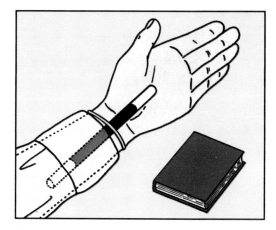

1 To prepare the trick, slide the magic wand up your left sleeve and secure it to your wrist with a rubber band. Make sure the rubber band holds the wand firmly against your arm, but is loose enough for you to slip the wand out easily.

2 To present the trick, hold the book in your right hand and point to it with your left forefinger. Tell the audience that you need to look up an unusual magic spell in your book.

3 Flip open the book with your right hand and place it into your left hand. Look down at the book and tell your audience that it says that you need a magic wand in order to perform your spell.

4 Reach inside the book with your right hand. Take hold of the wand and pull it out of your sleeve and into view. A big wand has been magically produced from a small book!

YOU WILL NEED
A magic wand
(see page 8)
A rubber band
A small book

RISING RING AND WAND

Here we show you how to perform not just one, but two mysterious tricks! Your audience will be amazed when you make a ring appear to move up and down your magic wand all by itself. Only you know that a length of fine thread is attached to the wand and to your clothes. When the thread is pulled taut, the ring rises up the wand. By using the same setup you can make the wand rise, too.

1 To prepare the trick, cut a length of thread about as long as your arm. Tie one end of the thread to the wand just below one of its ends. Tie the other end of the thread to a safety pin.

YOU WILL NEED

A magic wand
(see page 8)
Fine black thread
A small safety pin
A ring

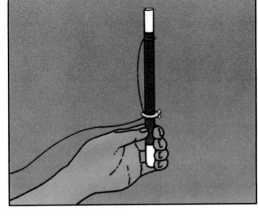

3 To present the trick, borrow a ring from a volunteer. Stand facing your audience so that they won't see the thread against your clothing. Take the wand in your left hand with the threaded end at the top and drop the ring over the wand. The ring will drop to the bottom of the wand, taking the thread down with it.

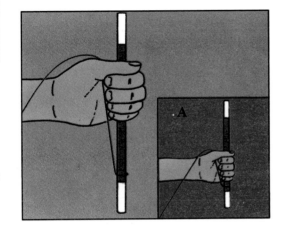

5 You can make the wand rise, too. To do this, push the threaded end of the wand into your fist. Hold the wand loosely at the top and move it away from your body. As you do this, the wand will rise up in your hand.

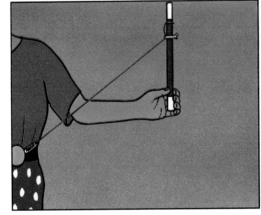

4 Move the wand away from your body so that the thread is pulled taut, and the ring will rise up the wand in a mysterious manner.

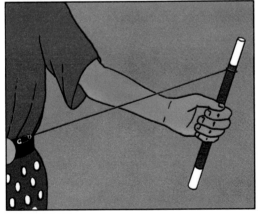

2 Pin the thread to your waist on the left side of your body. Make sure the safety pin is hidden under your belt or in a fold of clothing. Tuck the wand under your right arm.

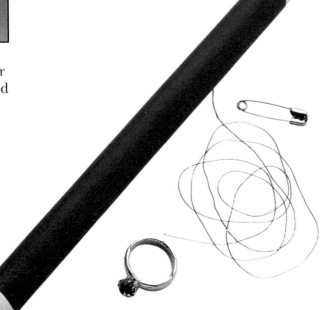

MAGIC BOX

The magic box is a very handy piece of equipment that can be used for many tricks. Use it to make items such as silk scarves disappear and then reappear, and to change one small item for another. Here we show you how to make your own magic box; on the next pages we show you how to use it.

1 To make the sides of the box, carefully cut four pieces of cardboard 4 by 7 inches.

2 For the box flap, cut a piece of cardboard 3¾ by 7 inches. Next, cut another piece of cardboard 4¼ by 4¼ inches. This will be the base of the box. Trim it to fit when you tape the box together.

YOU WILL NEED

Thick cardboard
A ruler
Scissors
Poster paints and
    paintbrush
All-purpose glue
Giftwrap
    Tape

4 Tape the four sides together along the long edges to make a box, as shown. Make sure that the painted sides face inward. Tape the short edge of the flap to the center of the base, so that it can move back and forth like a hinge.

5 Smear glue around the bottom of the box. Insert the flap into the box and stick the base to the bottom of the box.

6 When the glue has dried, trim the base so that it fits neatly against the bottom of the box. Cover the box with giftwrap.

3 Paint both sides of the flap black and leave it to dry. Now paint black the inside surfaces of the four sides of the box, as well as the inside surface of the base. Leave them to dry in a safe place.

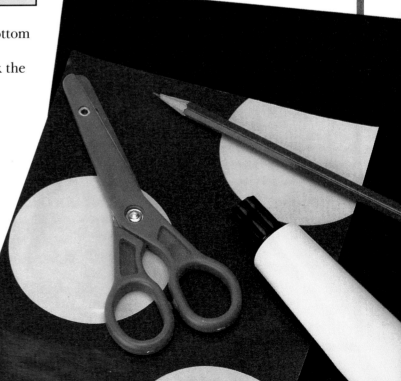

SILK SCARF MAGIC

Use your magic box to perform this mystifying trick. Show the box to your audience so that they can see that it's perfectly empty. Then say a couple of magic words and produce several brightly colored scarves from the "empty" box!

1 To prepare the trick, knot the three silk scarves together. Now conceal the scarves in the box under the flap, as shown.

2 To present the trick, hold the flap of the box down with the fingers of your right hand. Show the audience the inside of the box.

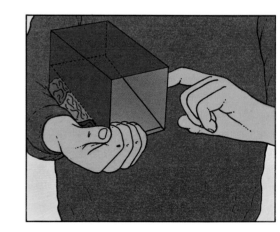

3 Tap the bottom and side of the box to show your audience that it is empty.

YOU WILL NEED

Magic Box
(see page 16)
Three silk scarves

4 Place the box in your left hand.
Tip the flap toward your body,
making sure that your audience
can't see what you're doing. Say a
magic word and pull the scarves out of
the box with a flourish.

THE LEAPING COMB

This amusing trick is a great way to open your magic show. Show the audience a perfectly normal comb in a case. What they don't know is that the comb is pushed down into the case on top of a rubber band. Ask your audience to join you in a comb countdown—"10, 9, 8, 7, 6, 5, 4, 3, 2, 1, zero! Blast off!" Release your grip on the case and watch the comb rocket upward!

YOU WILL NEED

Card
A comb
A ruler
Adhesive-backed paper
A rubber band
  2¾ inches long
Scissors
Double-sided tape
  A knitting needle

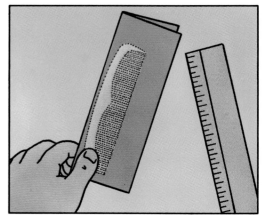

1 To make the comb case, fold the card in half. Hold the comb along the crease to measure the size the case will need to be. Cut the card so it is 1 inch wider and 1¼ inches longer than the comb.

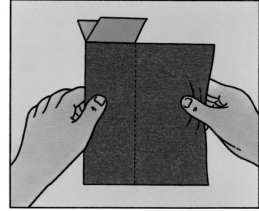

2 Make a cut 1¼ inches from the top of the card along the crease. Fold the cardboard down to make a collar, as shown. Cover the case, from the collar, with adhesive-backed paper, sealing the edges and the base. Do not cover the collar.

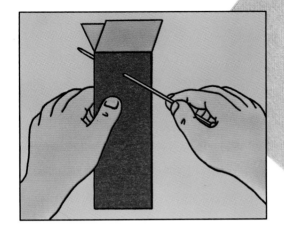

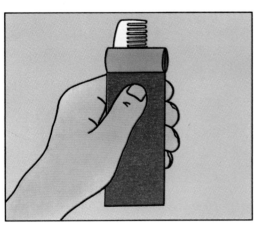

3 Make a hole through the case under the collar and 1 inch from the fold. Ask an adult to help you make the hole using a knitting needle or scissor points.

4 Cut the rubber band. Push one end through the hole at the front of the case and out through the hole at the back. Tie the ends of the rubber band together. Fold over the collar, to hide the knot, and stick in place with double-sided tape.

5 To set up the trick, push the comb into the case onto the rubber band. Grip the case and the comb just below the collar. Release your grip and the comb will leap into the air.

SAFETY TIP: *Make sure an adult helps you when using sharp scissors.*

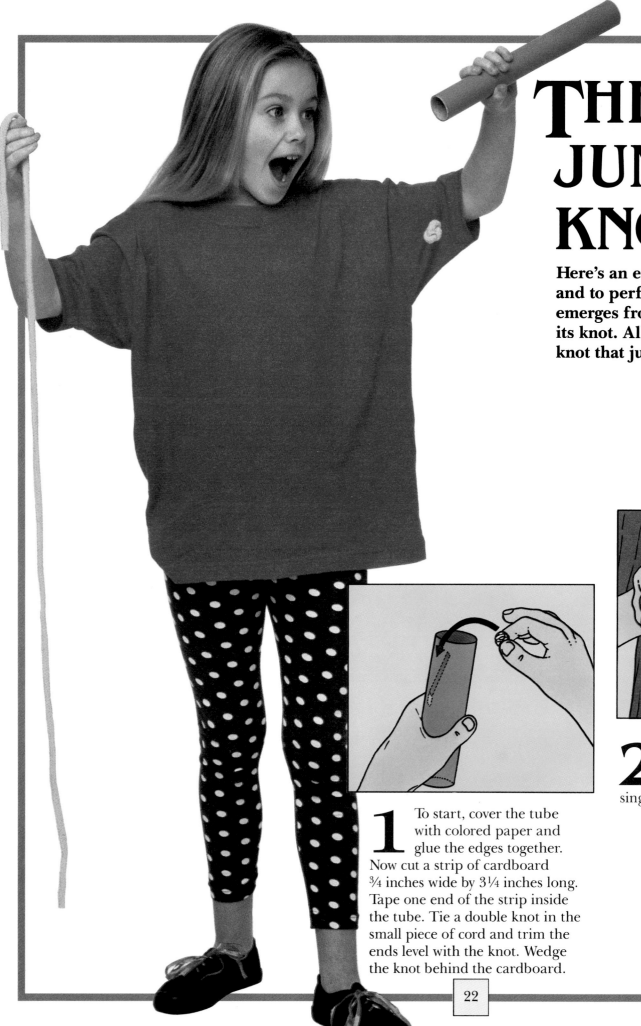

THE JUMPING KNOT

Here's an easy trick that is fun to prepare and to perform. A knotted piece of cord emerges from a cardboard tube without its knot. All you have to do is find the knot that jumped off the cord.

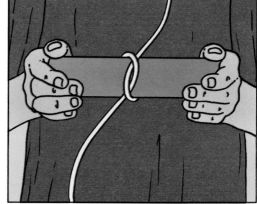

1 To start, cover the tube with colored paper and glue the edges together. Now cut a strip of cardboard ¾ inches wide by 3¼ inches long. Tape one end of the strip inside the tube. Tie a double knot in the small piece of cord and trim the ends level with the knot. Wedge the knot behind the cardboard.

2 To perform the trick, hold the tube as shown. Ask a volunteer to tie the long piece of cord in a single knot around the tube.

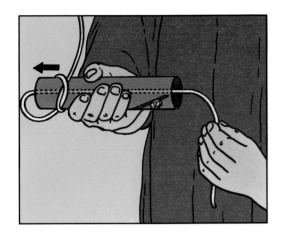

3 Slide the knot to the end of the tube and feed one end of the cord through the tube. (You will have to find out which end through trial and error.)

YOU WILL NEED

A long paper towel tube
Colored paper
All-purpose glue
Scrap cardboard
A ruler; scissors
Double-sided tape
A small piece of cord for the knot
36 inches of cord

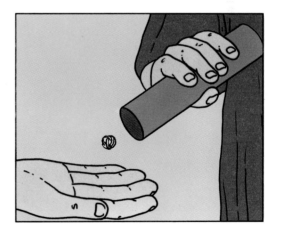

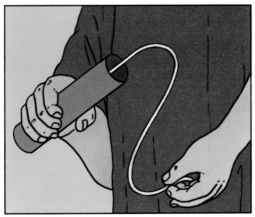

4 Grip the knot, slide it off the end of the tube, and push it into the tube.

5 Without disturbing the hidden knot wedged inside the tube, pull the rope out the other end of the tube. The rope will emerge unknotted. Tell your audience that the knot has vanished—or has it?

6 Carefully tap the tube to loosen the wedged knot and tip it out. Tell your audience that you have found the knot that jumped off the cord!

THE WONDER WIZARD

Make flat objects like coins, buttons, and postage stamps disappear into thin air with the help of the Wonder Wizard. The secret of this trick is to use the same color felt to cover the mouth of the tumbler and for the mat. When the tumbler is placed over a flat object on the mat, the object will seem to disappear.

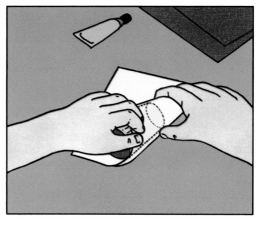

1 To prepare the trick, glue the circle of orange felt to the mouth of the tumbler. Now wrap the yellow cardboard around the tumbler to form a cone. Hold the cardboard in place with tape.

YOU WILL NEED
Scissors; all-purpose glue
A ruler
A plastic tumbler
A circle of orange felt cut to fit mouth of tumbler
Thin yellow cardboard; tape
Scraps of colored paper
Piece of orange felt (18 by 12 inches)
A coin

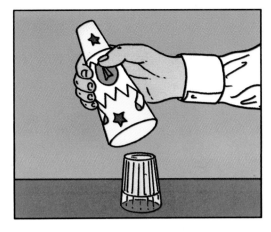

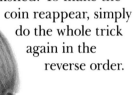

5 Lift off the wizard leaving the tumbler behind. The felt circle will hide the coin, which will appear to have vanished. To make the coin reappear, simply do the whole trick again in the reverse order.

4 Slip the wizard over the tumbler and stand both over the coin. Blow gently into the figure and say some magic words.

2 Trim the base of the cone so it stands up around the upside-down tumbler. Now decorate the cone to look like a wizard. Cut a beard, hat, and arms from colored paper, following the photograph, and glue to the cone. Add face details and stick red stars to the cone.

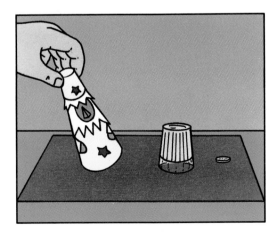

3 To perform the trick, set the tumbler face-down next to the wizard and coin on the felt mat.

THE VANISHING PENCIL

If you have a couple of tiny pencil stubs in your pencil box, don't throw them away! You can use them for this vanishing-pencil trick. You don't need to save this trick just for shows; it can be done anywhere. You can prepare it ahead of time and carry it with you to entertain people at school, on a long train or bus trip, or anywhere you can think of!

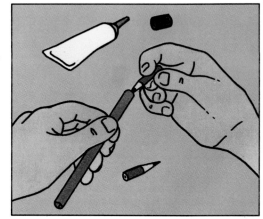

2 Take the two pencil stubs and glue them into the ends of the empty tube, as shown. This will be your dummy pencil. Hide the real pencil behind your collar.

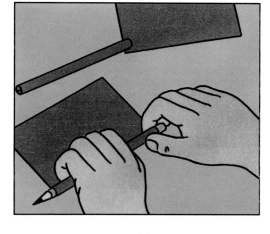

1 To prepare this trick, wrap some shiny paper around the full-sized pencil to make a tube. Secure the overlapped edges with glue. Slide the tube off the pencil. Repeat to make another tube, but this time glue the shiny paper to the pencil.

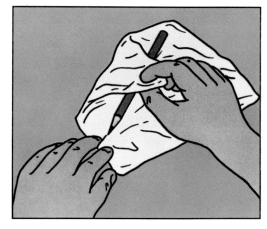

3 To present your trick, show the dummy pencil to your audience and wrap it in tissue paper. Tap the end of the pencil on a table to prove that it is solid.

YOU WILL NEED

Shiny paper
A full-sized pencil
All-purpose glue
Two pencil stubs
Tissue paper
Scissors

4 Say that you will now make the pencil vanish, and say some magic words. Screw up the tissue with a flourish and toss it in the air. The pencil stubs and the paper tube will be hidden in the tissue paper. Tuck the tissue paper in your pocket.

5 While your audience is still trying to work out how you made the pencil disappear, bring out the solid pencil from behind your collar.

THE MONEYMAKER

Here is a useful magician's skill that will dumbfound your audience. It lets you produce coins seemingly from thin air. Professional magicians usually take years to learn this technique, but using the shortcut shown here, you can learn the trick in just a few minutes.

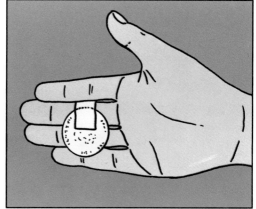

2 Hold the tab in position between the first and second fingers of your right hand. With the coin hanging down, as shown, and with the back of your hand facing the audience, the coin cannot be seen.

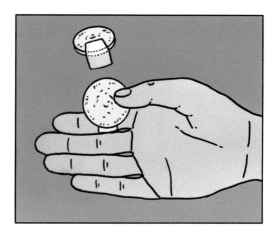

1 To prepare the trick, fasten a tab of tape to one of the coins. The tab should be long enough to be held between your fingers, as shown, without it showing on the other side of your hand.

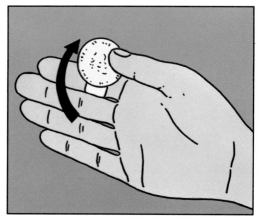

3 By putting your thumb under the coin and flipping it up, the coin looks as if it has been plucked from the air.

4 When you have practiced for a while, you will be ready to present your trick. Before you start, hide some coins in the top hat. To perform the trick, hold your hand over the hat, with the coin in the down position. Flip up the coin, as if you had "caught" it in the air, remove your thumb, and pretend to let the coin fall into the hat.

YOU WILL NEED
Twelve large coins
Clear tape
A top hat (see page 10)
A small bowl

5 Pretend to "catch" a number of coins from the air and "drop" them one at a time into the hat. Finish by tipping out the coins previously hidden in the hat into the bowl, to "prove" you really did throw the coins into the hat.

BELIEVE IT OR KNOT

Watch the wooden beads fall to the floor while leaving the cords mysteriously intact. The secret lies in the way the beads are threaded and knotted onto the cords. Practice this trick well before showing your friends.

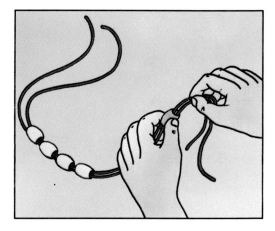

1 Fold each length of cord in half. Push the center of one piece through a bead and out the other side. Take the center of the other piece of cord and push it through the loop sticking out of the bead. Pull the loops back into the bead, as shown in diagram A.

2 Thread the remaining four beads onto the cord, two on either side of the center bead, as shown. To present the trick, show the bead necklace to your audience and ask for a volunteer to hold the ends of the cords.

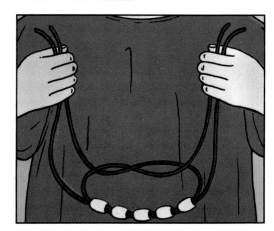

3 Say that the beads are securely threaded onto the cord, but to make sure, you will take a cord from each of your volunteer's hands and tie them in a single knot. Make sure that after tying the knot the cord from the right hand is returning to the left hand and the cord from the left hand is going to the right hand.

4 With your volunteer still holding the cords, cover the bead necklace with a handkerchief, as shown. Explain that you will attempt to remove the beads from the cord.

5 Reach under the handkerchief and release the wedged center bead, and all the others will follow. Take away the handkerchief and hold up the cords to show your audience that they are still intact.

YOU WILL NEED

Five large beads
A ruler
Scissors
Two pieces of cord,
  24 inches long
A large handkerchief

CUP AND SPOON SORCERY

This mysterious trick is guaranteed to keep your audience guessing— so make sure you don't reveal your secret. The cup and silk scarf stay suspended on the spoon by means of a cleverly concealed magnet.

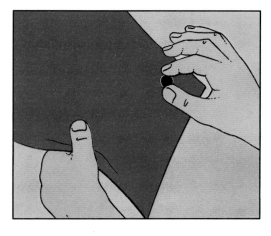

1 To prepare for the trick, stick the magnet 1½ inches from one corner of the silk scarf with double-sided tape.

2 Hold the scarf in your right hand, with your thumb hiding the magnet, as shown. Show the empty plastic cup to your audience with your left hand.

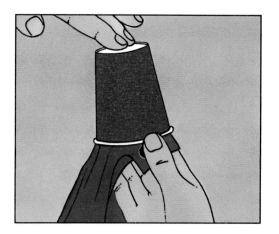

3 Place the cup over your right hand. Make sure that the corner of the scarf with the magnet attached is outside the cup.

4 Holding the rim of the cup with the fingers and thumb of your right hand, flip the cup over so that the scarf hangs over the mouth of the cup. Tuck the silk into the cup with your left hand.

5 Place the cup on your left palm, allowing the magnet to hang outside the cup. Make sure that the magnet faces you and not your audience. Lower the handle of the spoon into the cup, remove your supporting hand, and the cup and scarf will remain suspended on the spoon.

YOU WILL NEED

A lightweight silk scarf
A small magnet
A ruler
Double-sided tape
A plastic cup
A large metal spoon

THE PENETRATING PENCIL

The penetrating pencil can be performed wherever you have a pencil and a handkerchief. By making a special fold in the handkerchief, you can make the pencil appear to fall straight through the handkerchief as if it had magically penetrated the fabric.

1 Drape the handkerchief over your left hand, as shown. Allow more of the fabric to hang down on the audience's side.

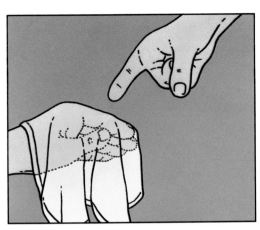

2 Push your right forefinger into the handkerchief, between the thumb and forefinger of your left hand, to make a well.

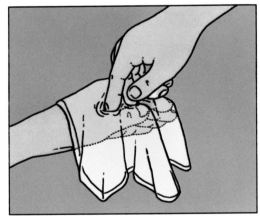

3 At the same time, secretly make a fold in the handkerchief with the second finger of your right hand, as shown.

4 Now pick up a pencil (or pen) and announce to your audience that you will make it drop straight through the handkerchief. Push the pencil into the secret fold. Your audience will think it is going into the well, but the pencil will fall to the ground, penetrating the handkerchief.

YOU WILL NEED
A pencil (or pen)
A large handkerchief

SHIRT SHOCK

This is a stunt that needs some secret preparation with a trusted friend well before the show begins. When you whip off your friend's shirt, shout a magic word to get even more reaction from your audience.

1 To prepare this trick, get your helper to remove his shirt before the show. Slip the shirt over his shoulders and fasten two or three buttons at the neck. Button the cuffs around his wrists, as shown.

2 Put your friend's sweater or jacket back on and arrange the shirt so that everything looks perfectly normal.

3 To perform the trick, invite your friend to come and help you and seat him on a chair. Tell the audience you can use your magic powers to make a person feel colder. Ask your friend to unbutton his shirt at the neck and wrists.

YOU WILL NEED

A friend with a shirt and a sweater who will be in on the secret
A chair

5 Much to the surprise of your audience, the shirt will come away free. Say "*Now* do you feel any colder?" Arrange with your friend to act embarrassed, grab the shirt, and run off.

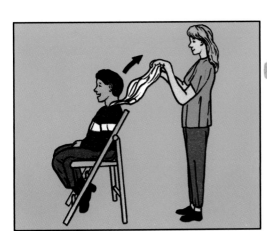

4 Wave your hands around your friend's head as if you were hypnotizing him. Ask if he feels any colder. Your friend should say "no." Then suddenly take hold of his shirt at the collar and pull it upward.

RING-IN RING-ON

All magicians know that the hand is sometimes quicker than the eye. This means that you can make your audience think they are seeing something that looks impossible but you know it is simply a trick of the hand. In this trick, you can convince the audience that a solid plastic ring has threaded itself onto a length of rope, even though the two ends of the rope were in full view the whole time.

1 Set your table as shown above. The ends of the two ropes must be kept hidden by the hat, ready to be picked up and held to look like one piece of rope. Stand behind the table with the hat on your right-hand side.

2 Pick up the pieces of rope, holding the ends of the short and long pieces in your right hand, as shown, so that the two pieces look like one length of rope. Lower the center of the rope into the hat.

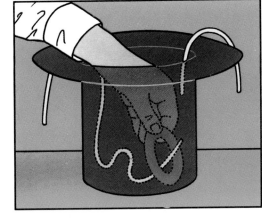

5 Mutter a magic word and pick up the two secret ends of the rope in your right hand, as shown, and the other end in your left hand. Pull the rope from the hat to reveal that the ring has penetrated the rope.

3 When your hands touch the edge of the hat, secretly drop the right hand end of the long piece of rope into the hat. Drape the left-hand end and the short piece of rope over the brim, as shown.

4 Ask a member of the audience to hold the plastic ring and to make sure it is solid. Place the ring into the hat, secretly slipping it over the end of the long rope.

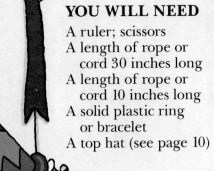

YOU WILL NEED

A ruler; scissors
A length of rope or
cord 30 inches long
A length of rope or
cord 10 inches long
A solid plastic ring
or bracelet
A top hat (see page 10)

LAZY LINKING CHAINS

This is a spectacular trick that will go off with a bang! Magicians have always stunned audiences by making solid objects link up as if by magic. Here we show you how to make separate links of a chain appear to join together to form one long chain.

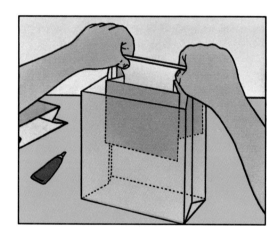

1 To prepare this trick, cut one of the paper bags in half. Glue the bottom half of the bag to the inside back of the second bag, as shown, to make a secret inner bag.

2 Place the chain in the bottom of the full-sized bag and the links in the plastic tumbler.

3 To perform the trick, hold up the bag and drop the chain links from the tumbler into the inner bag. Drop the links in one at a time to show that they are really separate.

4 Close the inner bag, and blow up the large outer bag. Twist the neck to keep the air in.

5 Pop the large outer bag and pull out the long chain. The separate links will remain hidden in the inner bag.

41

MAGIC GLASSES

This trick is guaranteed to stun your audience. Tell them that you have found a pair of magic glasses that give you the power to see through solid objects. They may laugh when you show them a pair of plastic scissors, but the last laugh will be yours!

1 To prepare the trick, smear glue on one side of the coin. Lay the hair across it and leave to dry in a safe place.

YOU WILL NEED

All-purpose glue
A coin
A human hair
Three colorful bottle caps
Plastic scissors
A ruler

3 To perform the trick, show the scissors to your audience and tell them that they are really a pair of magic glasses that enable you to see through solid objects. Now turn your back to the audience. Ask a volunteer to cover the coin with one of the three caps and mix them around.

4 Turn around and peer through the scissors, as if they were a pair of glasses. Look for the tell-tale hair and reveal the coin.

2 When the glue is dry, turn the coin glue side down and cover it with a bottle cap. Cut the hair so it sticks out from under the cap by about ⅛ inch.

SCARF SORCERY

All you need for this trick is a silk scarf, some black thread, and a chair. With some slick hand movements and a little bit of practice, you can make the scarf appear to pass right through the back of the chair. Make sure your audience sits facing the front of the chair so that they can't see your secret hand movements.

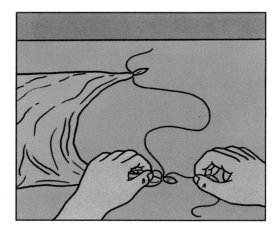

1 To prepare this trick, take the silk scarf and tie a length of black thread to two diagonally opposite corners, as shown.

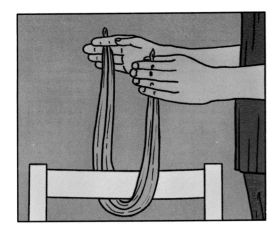

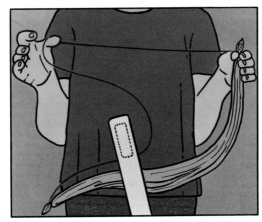

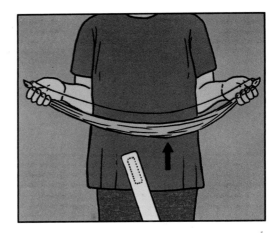

2 To perform the trick, pass the scarf through the chairback and hold it up by the threaded ends with the thumb and first finger of your left hand, and the first and second fingers of your right hand.

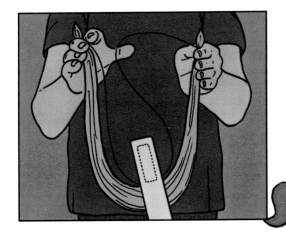

4 Release the scarf from your right hand and at the same time pull your hands upward and outward. The released end of the scarf will be pulled by the thread around the chair and back to your right fingers.

5 Your audience won't be able to see you release the scarf from your right hand, as this movement will be covered by the front end of the scarf and your left hand. All they will see is the scarf appear to pass through the back of the chair.

3 Lower and raise the scarf a few times so that it touches the chair. On the final down movement, slip your right thumb under the left-hand end of the thread, as shown.

YOU WILL NEED

A dark-colored scarf
A length of strong, but fine, black thread
An open-backed chair

SLIPPERY SILK

The rope is knotted to the silk scarf, but the silk is also knotted to the rope. Your friends' eyes will pop out when you pull the scarf away from the rope with its knot still intact.

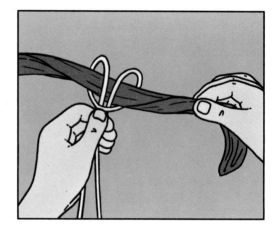

1 To present this trick, pick up the rope and tug it to show that it is intact. Fold it in two. Make a loop in the rope, as shown, but tell your audience that you have formed a "knot" in the middle of the rope. Take the silk scarf and pass it through the loop or "knot" as shown.

2 Pull the "knot" tight and show your audience that the rope is knotted to the scarf. Tell your audience that you will now tie the scarf to the rope. Tie a single loose knot with the scarf, as shown.

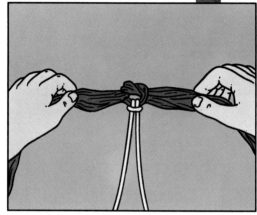

3 Hold the rope about 12 inches on either side of the "knot" and tug the ends as if to show all is genuine. In fact this move upsets the knots and causes a large silk loop to form at the center of the scarf. The scarf is now ready to be removed.

4 Put your left foot on one end of the rope and pull it taut with your left hand. Take hold of the scarf by the loop at the center and slide it, with a sawing action, up and down the rope.

5 Pull the silk scarf sharply away from the rope and it will come free, still knotted!

YOU WILL NEED

A ruler; scissors
A piece of soft
rope 6 feet long
A thin silk scarf
18 inches square

CUT AND RESTORED ROPE

This is a classic trick that will take you no time at all to perfect. A long piece of rope is cut in half and then magically restored by tying some clever knots.

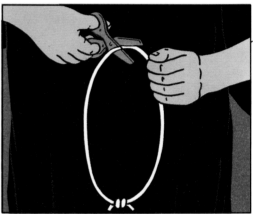

2 To present the trick, show the rope to your audience. They will think it is a piece of rope tied with a knot. Cut through the glued join with the scissors, and tie the ends together in a knot.

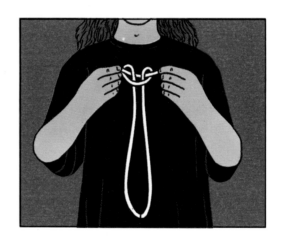

1 To prepare the trick, glue the ends of the long piece of rope together to form a circle. Leave to dry. Form a loop in the rope on the opposite side of the join, as shown. Insert the small piece of rope into the loop to look like a knot. Pull the rope to tighten the knot.

3 Hold the rope with the real knot in your right hand and the dummy knot in your left hand. Ask an audience member to call out left or right.

4 If "Left!" is called out, say "I'll untie my knot." If "Right" is called out, say "I'll untie your knot!" Either way, untie the real knot. Take hold of the dummy knot, and trim the ends of the short piece of rope close to the loops.

5 Hold the rope in your hands with the trimmed dummy knot in the center. Say a magic word and pull. The knot will fly off, leaving the rope completely restored!

CHOOSE A CARD

Here is a clever mind reading trick that is guaranteed to baffle your friends. With the help of some trick cards and a special "scissor" move, you will be able to read the mind of your volunteer to reveal the card he was thinking about.

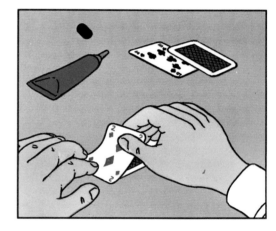

1 To prepare the trick, glue two cards, say the two of diamonds and the eight of clubs, back to back. This is called a "double-facer." Now glue two cards face to face. This is called a "double-backer."

2 Hold the cards between the thumb and fingers of your right hand, with the "double-backer" on top and the eight of clubs underneath, as shown. To practice the special "scissor" move, turn your hand over to show the other side of the cards, and at the same time push your thumb to the left and your forefinger to the right in a scissor movement. This moves the double-facer across and allows the two of diamonds to be shown. Reverse these moves when you turn your hand back again.

3 To present the trick, show the cards to your audience using the special scissor move and then drop them into a top hat. Ask someone to think of either card and tell him you will read his mind and reveal which card he was thinking of.

5 Now ask your helper which card he thought of. If he names the card that is face up in the hat, simply tilt the hat to show the card. If he names the other side of the card, reach into the hat and bring out the card with the side he named face up.

4 Reach inside the hat and take out the double-backer. At the same time sneak a look in the hat and note which side of the double-facer is showing. Hold up the double-backer. Say "It's not this one" and place the card in your pocket.

YOU WILL NEED

Four playing cards
All-purpose glue
A top hat (see page 10)

THE UNTYING HANDKERCHIEF

Everyone will be amazed and amused by the snakelike antics of this animated handkerchief. Only you know that a length of fine thread is secretly attached to the handkerchief, so that when you pull the thread the handkerchief will unravel itself from its knot.

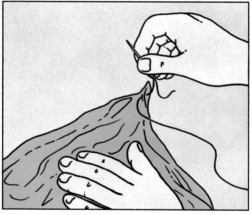

1 To prepare the trick, cut a length of thread that is long enough to reach from your feet to just above your waist. Stitch one end of the thread to a corner of the handkerchief and tie the other end to your right shoe.

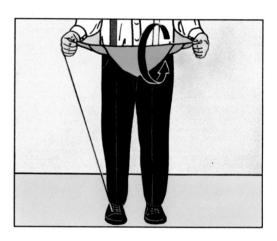

2 To perform the trick, hold the handkerchief between your hands with the threaded end in your right hand. Roll the scarf up with a forward circular motion, as shown.

3 Form the scarf into a loop, as shown in diagram A. Pull the threaded end of the scarf through the loop, as shown in diagram B.

YOU WILL NEED

Strong fine thread
and a needle
A silk handkerchief
(or scarf)

4 Pull the knot a little tighter, as shown in diagram A. Now, holding the unthreaded end of the scarf, pull the scarf upward, as shown in diagram B.

5 As the thread is pulled taut, the threaded end of the scarf will snake upward through the knot and untie itself.

53

NO CHOICE

This clever card trick shows you how to make a member of your audience select the card that you want chosen. The secret lies in the way you set up the cards before you begin.

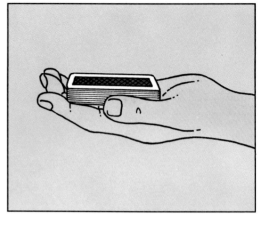

2 To perform the trick, take the pack of cards and hold them facedown in your left hand. Take care not to reveal the faceup cards at the bottom of the pack.

1 To prepare the trick, first take any card and place it faceup on the bottom of the pack. Now put the card you want your volunteer to choose (for example, the nine of spades) faceup under the first card, as shown.

YOU WILL NEED

A pack of cards
A large handkerchief

3 Explain that you are going to ask a volunteer to cut the pack and then select the top card from the cards left in your hand. Tell your audience that you will cover the pack of cards with a handkerchief so that you will not be able to see your volunteer cutting the pack.

4 Now ask a volunteer to feel through the handkerchief and cut the pack. As she removes the cards and the handkerchief, secretly flip the pack over in your hand. The nine of spades will now be on the top of the pack.

5 Offer the cards to your volunteer and ask her to select the top card. At the same time tell her that you already know it will be the nine of spades—which, of course, it is!

MAGIC SCISSORS

Here is a super card trick based on "No Choice" (see page 54). Your audience will be baffled when you produce cutout representations of the cards they have chosen. Only you know that the cards have been secretly set up beforehand so that your volunteers select the cards that you want them to!

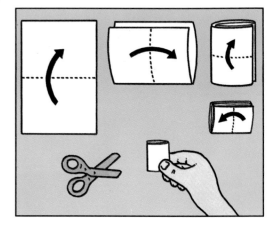

1 To prepare this trick, take the pack of cards and place any card faceup on the bottom of the pack. Now place three cards—the eight of hearts, the eight of spades, and the four of diamonds – faceup under the first card at the bottom of the pack. Memorize the order of the cards. Following steps 2-5 of "No Choice," have three volunteers select the cards, but ask them not to tell you what they have selected.

2 Show a sheet of paper to your audience and fold it neatly in half four times. Explain that with the help of your magic scissors you will try to discover which three cards have been selected.

3 Ask the volunteer who chose the first card (the eight of hearts) to concentrate on the card he selected. Carefully cut out the shape shown above from your folded piece of paper. Ask your volunteer what the card is and open out the folded paper. It will have eight cutout hearts.

4 Refold the cut piece of paper, and ask your second volunteer to concentrate on the card he selected. Now cut out the shape shown above from the paper. Ask your volunteer to name his card and open out the paper to reveal the eight of spades.

5 Now you come to your last volunteer. Refold the paper once again and ask your helper to concentrate on his card. Cut out the shape shown above and ask for the name of the third card. When he says "the four of diamonds," hesitate and make a face. Everyone will think you have made a mistake and cut out another eight. You haven't, of course, so smile and open the paper to reveal the four of diamonds.

YOU WILL NEED

A sheet of paper
A pack of cards
A large handkerchief
Scissors

THE MAGIC ELEVATOR

Perform this gravity-defying feat to delighted gasps from your audience. Your friends will not be able to work out how the white spool of thread ends up on top of the red ones. Only you know the secret.

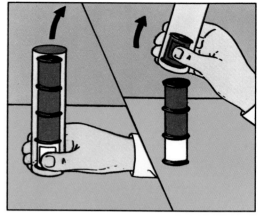

2 Now learn the secret move. Cover the spools with the tube. Hold the tube with your fingers at the front and your thumb over the hole; lift off the tube. When the bottom of the tube is level with the lower edge of the top spool, push your thumb into the hole and pick up the spool. Place the tube next to the three spools.

1 To make the magic tube, cut the cardboard tube so that it is just slightly taller than the height of the four spools of thread. Cover the tube with adhesive-backed paper. Cut a hole in the back of the tube about ¾ inch square.

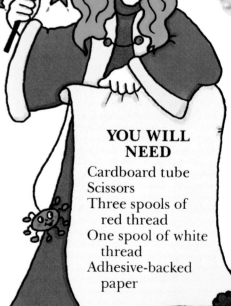

YOU WILL NEED

Cardboard tube
Scissors
Three spools of red thread
One spool of white thread
Adhesive-backed paper

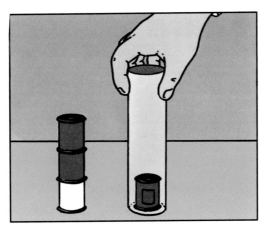

3 To set up the trick, stack the three red spools on top of the white spool. Cover the spools with the tube with the hole facing you. Lift off the tube "stealing" the top red spool. Place the tube and the spool on the table. You are ready to perform the trick. Tell the audience that the white spool is the "elevator" and the red spools are floors one and two. Explain that you will make the elevator rise to the first floor. Take the white spool from the stack and drop it into the tube on top of the hidden red spool. Now drop in the other two red spools.

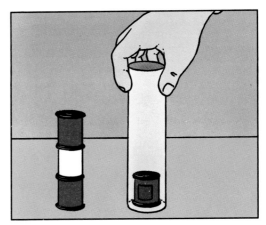

4 Say some magic words and pick up the tube, once again "stealing" the top red spool. Put the tube and spool on the table. The white spool has moved to the first floor.

5 Explain that you are now going to move the elevator to the second floor. Take the red spool from the stack and drop it into the tube on top of the secret red spool. Now drop the white spool and then the remaining red spool into the tube. Abracadabra! Take off the tube, once again "stealing" the top spool. The white spool is at the top of the stack on the second floor.

THE BOX JUMPER

Here is a dramatic trick that is often performed on stage and television by professional magicians. Your audience is shown what seems to be a perfectly empty cardboard box made up of two three-sided "screens." They won't believe it when you clap your hands and your assistant pops out of the box.

1 To prepare the trick, cut the top and bottom flaps, and one whole side from each carton to make two three-sided screens, as shown.

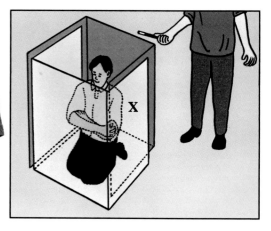

2 Arrange the screens to form an enclosed box, as shown, with your assistant hidden inside. Notice the side marked X.

YOU WILL NEED

2 large cardboard cartons (freezer or washing machine boxes are best)

Scissors

A magic wand (see page 8)

4 Now pull out the carton your assistant had been hiding in, and swing it around to show your audience. Place the carton in position at the rear of the front carton as shown.

5 Clap your hands, wave your magic wand, and your assistant will pop out of the box.

3 To present the trick, open side X slightly toward your audience. Pull out the rear carton and swing it round to show your audience. Move the carton to your left by the side of the other carton so that it slightly overlaps the side marked X. While you do this, your assistant moves unseen into the (now) front carton.

THE FLOATING LADY

One of the most exciting tricks that a magician can do is to levitate a human being. To "levitate" means to rise or float in the air without anything or anyone helping or giving support. Now you can do this famous trick in your magic show, too, with the help of a friend who is good at keeping secrets. All you need is a large sheet and time to practice.

1 To perform the trick, stand facing your audience and ask your friend to lie on her back on the floor in front of you.

2 Cover your friend with the sheet. As you do this, hold the sheet in front of your friend for just a couple of seconds, so that she is blocked from view. As soon as she is out of sight, she quickly turns face downward.

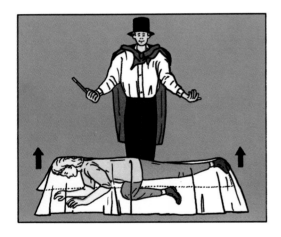

3 Wave your magic wand and say a magic word. This is the cue for your friend to start to rise upward. She does this by sticking one leg out straight and raising herself up on her hands and her other leg.

YOU WILL NEED

A bedsheet or a long length of fabric

A magic wand (see page 8)

4 Your friend should continue to rise up slowly until she is about 24 inches above the ground. Say another magic word as the cue for her to descend slowly to the floor.

INDEX

ACKNOWLEDGMENTS

The author and publishers would like to thank Waddingtons Games Ltd. for permission to photograph their playing cards.